PRAISE FOR

BELIEVE WHAT YOU CAN

———

"*Believe What You Can* overflows with rich lines and vivid images, as the poet laureate of West Virginia speaks to classic concerns of loving the land, struggling to thrive, and holding on to what can be believed."

—Ron Houchin,
author of *The Man Who Saws Us In Half: Poems*

"Harshman's poetic sophistication is clear and shows the insight and wisdom of an experienced poet who treats the forces of death, disruption, and dissonance with the seriousness and humor they deserve."

—Eddy Pendarvis,
author of *Like the Mountains of China*
and *Ghost Dance Poems*

"'I never lie but like to tell a story,' Marc Harshman's canny, slightly unreliable narrator tells us, and every story in these poems unsettles our 'tawdry certainties.' To enter this work is to remain open to the haphazard, the lopsided, the fragile, and the bracing details that tell our times as we both know and fear them. *Believe What You Can* is an astonishing and generous book that gives a credible 'map of true witness.'"

—Maggie Anderson,
author of *Windfall: New and Selected Poems*
and *Dear All*

for Bean —

Marc Harshman

• • • • •

Believe What
You Can

POEMS

"Believe
what
11.14.17 y ou
can!"

VANDALIA PRESS • MORGANTOWN • 2016

For Ken Sullivan

CONTENTS

——

I

Yew Piney Mountain   3
Coal Country   5
Learning to Read   8
Return Ticket   9
Holding On   12
Worries   14
Dreaming the Farm   15
Grandmother at the Dressmakers'   18
Somewhere   20
Postcard   21
Seven League Boots   23
Aunt Helen   25

II

Evidence   29
Finding the Lost   30
How We Go Missing   32
Carrion Chance   33
Where No One Else Can Go   35
Pietà   37

A Moon Somewhere Else   40
Pink Ladies   41
Where They Can't Find Us   43

III

Not Quite Haphazardly   47
These   49
Fucked   50
The Innocent   52
Time Traveler in Greenville, Ohio   53
Broken   55
Not with a Bang   58
Anti-Monotony   60
Normal   61
Vehicular   62

IV

It Was Told   67
Cold Morning   70
Stone   71
Winter into Spring   73
Late September   75
Recoveries   76
Peter's Mountain   78
Monastery   80

Jackson Pollock and the Starlings,
    Moundsville, West Virginia   81
The News   82
Clark Hill   83
You Could Live   84
And Fly   85
Beyond   86
With No Questions   87

Reading Notes   89
About the Author   91

ACKNOWLEDGMENTS

———

I wish to thank the editors of the following publications, where some of these poems first appeared:

Appalachian Heritage: "Winter into Spring"; *Bitter Oleander*: "Learning to Read" (originally "Promised"); *Blueline*: "Clark Hill" (originally "Wind Ridge"); *Bryant Literary Review*: "Monastery" (forthcoming); *Chariton Review*: "Time Traveler in Greenville, Ohio" (originally "Lowell Thomas in Greenville, Ohio"); *Cleaver*: "Fucked" and "The Innocent"; *Drafthorse Literary Journal*: "Pink Ladies"; *First Intensity*: "Not Quite Haphazardly"; *Hamilton Stone Review*: "Seven League Boots"; *Innisfree Poetry Journal*: "Pietà"; *Literary Bohemian*: "Postcard"; *Poetry Salzburg Review*: "Return Ticket"; *Scintilla*: "Stone" and "Recoveries"; *Still: The Journal*: "With No Questions," "Stone," and "Grandmother at the Dressmakers'"; *Storm Cellar*: "Holding On" (forthcoming); *Words* (Thomas More College): "Peter's Mountain" (originally "Snowshoe")

"Jackson Pollock and the Starlings ..." was first published in the *Anthology of Appalachian Writers* (Shepherdstown, WV: Shepherd University, 2009).

The poems "Normal" and "Anti-Monotony" were written in reply to an invitation by the artist Donald

Swartzentruber to contribute poetic responses to his series of works entitled *Totem Triptychs*. They may be seen at http://swartzentruber.com/index.htm.

"Dreaming the Farm," "Where No One Else Can Go," "A Moon Somewhere Else," "These," and "Late September" were first published in *Green-Silver and Silent* (Huron, OH: Bottom Dog Press, 2012). Periodical publication of "These" in *Anglican Theological Review* and "Late September" in *Third Wednesday*.

"Evidence" was first published in the chapbook *All That Feeds Us: The West Virginia Poems* (Charlestown, WV: Quarrier Press, 2013).

Thank you to Cheryl, spouse, friend, and eagle-eyed reader of English prose.

Thank you to Anna Egan Smucker who has, again, read them all and offered intelligence and much needed criticism.

Thank you to Maggie Anderson for friendship, support, and an invaluable reading of this manuscript.

I

If you don't know the trees you may be lost in the forest,
but if you don't know the stories you may be lost in life.
—Siberian Elder

YEW PINEY MOUNTAIN

for Doug Van Gundy

———

In the old fiddle tunes there is always
    a stream running—rocks and roaring cascades.
In the best tunes, in the Yew Piney Mountains,
    there's a rising wind, a young girl's whistling,
    a piper readying for battle.
And someone's on their death bed—true enough.
And a cat is screaming, strangled
    with midnight desire—sure.
And somewhere granddad is mumbling to himself—
    granted.
But there are, as well, frothy backwashes
    and somewhere above, little grace-notes
    echoing within the bell jar of quiet.
In the woods behind all this silver singing
    a child adventures through a swift-settling fog,
    the oak and hickories mute with secrets.
There are no easy endings, and yet
    the pulse keeps ticking where the faceless player
    predictably returns the up-and-down
    ladder of seconds and days and years.
The stream, of course, keeps speaking
    its many tongues, running syllables and notes
    loose and free over its ancient bed.

But is it running with whiskey,
    or running with fire,
    or just now simply running with spring,
    icy on this first warm day,
    running only to run, to run away?

COAL COUNTRY

The fires follow the spine of the mountain
       into the night where clouds
       part and surrender.
Within the abandoned hour, bells begin
       clapping their singular tongues.
An owl climbs the restive stillness onto a soap box
       where the moon,
       pensive and contrite,
       waits with its scissors and bowl.
Inside a house, two lights on downstairs, the phone rings.
A mosquito threads the dark
       with its delicate and voracious heat.
The tap drips.
A pale fish jumps in an old, green pond.
A slender flame leaps.
Grandmother holds the clock in her strong grip
       and won't let go
       as the stars steer their courses
       over the lost schools of the Saviour.
Beyond these little desolations, there is someone
       who has noticed, who knocks
       at that door, shouts, climbs through a window,
       turns off the tap,
       unlocks both the door

and grandmother's fingers, picks
up the phone, but, before answering, glances
back through the window
to where the shimmer on the pond lifts
its voice,
and so hears the silence,
feels a shiver
race round the globe.
Feels the flickering heat.
Asleep, we hear the buzzing draw near.
We shift, reach for comforts, try ignoring this summons,
this tolling of tongues, this conflagration of voices.
Grandmother is cold now, though smiling without her
corset.
Was he wrong to wake us?
The nightmares were salvific, our open hearts their kindling,
and the road ahead longer
than the histories to which we cling,
a hard road through these mountains
where lies have bred so long
even storytellers believe
the only magic still burning
lives in those wicked seams
next door to hell.

We impale the mosquito against the rusty screen.
The phone lies silent where we search the dream litter

left upon our lips, touch our fingers there, taste
the cold steel of the graveyard shovel.
A chisel. Soft, white stone. A message to be gotten out,
a few words to wind justice around silken arrows
meant for the heart, the true-believer's,
as he sits in his blind pew,
worshiping Alger and Murdoch,
and the last pebbles of coal stinking like brimstone.

LEARNING TO READ

Inside the forgotten room, a white sky lifts
its shoulders above craggy promontories
of book-lined shelves. A girl follows a string
of thread between shadows of ink. The clock
has lost its way and the dog sleeps
below an arching forest of mullioned windows.
It is not that anyone still waits.
The story began long ago and what they call
   adventure
is just this place, this day where the new sky begins
to mist over with tears and the lake's hissing surf
repeats for you, generously, what you already know.
Take heart. This room was once yours,
and you were promised a key. It will be found
and fit both your hand and the lock.
There is no trickery in this. You need only wait.
Perhaps tomorrow this very day will be waiting
for you, and, through these same windows,
you will watch orange birds
stitch these green libraries
back into song.

RETURN TICKET

for John Moore

———

John sat reading his Bible, a joint
in one hand, a glass of red,
cheap red, in the other, a tin of tuna
centering the table—our shared lunch—
he lifted his head, wondering—perhaps
I did, as well—whether
the two ends would ever meet, about
the tie that binds, whether the circle
would be unbroken, whether Bojangles
ever really danced, while Kitty purred
in one corner and I sat in the other
chanting the names of each pebble
we'd adopted in case of Kitty's demise.
We weren't the only ones in danger of overdosing:
the catnip flourishing under
the pot's frondy leaves had left her
comatose after her hour chasing circles.

A jolly chessboard sat on the floor.
A game of chance, I insisted, despite
his winning again and again.
He'd been to heaven, or so he told me,
and the return ticket he kept buried

9

in the drawer with condoms
and roach clips and blue rags.
But even the acid wouldn't dislodge
his itinerary or his visions.
Cards close to his chest, an old man
of the mountains at twenty-two.
I joined him for strolls through forests
we worshipped in the abstract
while scheming to get laid.
He won there, too. Despite his oddities,
he knew the talk and I never did.
The women flocked. I hid.
The cat died. The pebbles, though we tried
calling them by name, never warmed
to us and soon, names forgotten,
disappeared under the broom
onto College Street where the new children
never stopped arriving. He was legendary
by then and I'd gone straight, headed east.
It seemed a good direction to go.
He emptied his drawers and told me later
that the ticket had gone missing.
He had, however, saved one last pebble and
placing it on his tongue, found himself—
he swore to this—speaking like a cat
coherently summoning his pride to follow him
all the way to Maine and Indiana.

Maybe it's true. He's asked me about that ticket.
I never lie but sometimes, sometimes at night,
after a meal of tuna and wine, I like to tell a story.
And John, he shows up, every time, wings
at his shoulders, joint at his lips.

HOLDING ON

There was thunder building behind the mountain but
she was in no hurry and the air was so still she knew that
what storm would come was in no hurry, either. She swept
the porch, knelt to dead-head petunias her daughter had
sent in the spring. She undid a second button on her
blouse, could feel the sweat pool along the nape of her
neck. When it finally came, the breeze was delicious.
She sat and spread her legs and breathed: in . . . out . . .
—like yoga, she supposed. The garden was thriving this
year. The tomatoes, especially: her Brandywines big as
softballs. She hoped there would be no hail. The breeze
had already stopped. But she loved these moments of
heavy silence before a big storm. Earlier a jay had made
two sharp, scrying squawks from the shadows in the
tree line, but now a few crickets and the slow tumble of
the dryer behind her in the basement were all she could
hear. Funny to think they'd given her only a couple more
months, and yet she was sitting here as fully alive as she
felt anyone could ever feel. Sure, there was the dull ache
in her side, and she knew were it not for the meds, she'd
not sleep. But . . . she had the meds and she *would* sleep.
And she wouldn't, and wasn't . . . going to worry. The first
ripple of lightning had just filigreed the left flank of the
mountain like a flash for coming attractions and now here

was the breeze again. She went ahead and undid the rest of her buttons and slipped off her blouse. How good that was. She felt—she smiled to herself—impossibly, and yet delightfully, amorous. She undid her shorts and slipped them off, too. There would be storm and thunder, lightning, but there would be, as well, the familiar feel of her body—call it love, this holding on to life within the dull and predictable solemnities of death.

WORRIES

———

Brittle and wan
fronds of tall grass
slice the dry air
and the crumbs gather
moisture at night and mold
in the basement where
a woman rolls up her sleeves
and, free there of sweat, irons
shoe laces and ribbons
for the children's dolls who live
in the house unaware
of drought, of how meager
the crumbs are this year,
of what's happening beyond.

DREAMING THE FARM

1

A slow mile in heavy snow.
Steadily his shadow follows
under icy sunlight.

It will be a cow he's after,
down with calf—birthed or dead,
a clumsy, heavy job either
to get them or it, back or buried,
one or the other, or both.

He crests the rounded knob
and disappears, the sky
blinding with its blue frost.

2

It's maybe the pushing wind
I wouldn't want to face,
or the loss of time
from other chores.
I wouldn't think it's sentiment
when he covers his cheeks
with his hands
in the raw, burning air.

But in the moment
when he pulls the still calf
out of the blood-seared womb
and feels the loss, the cooling stick of skin,
what is that, who
are these animals—this one
dead, the other, too,
to follow soon, bleeding—what
are they to him?

3

Always the promise
and never
is it certain, the dream
of spring ending
so far out of season.

Don't tell me
he doesn't see it this way—
I know that.
And he does.

How much the natural round
predictably avers death
he should know, and does,

and doesn't, and this one lesson fails
predictably.

The clouds have risen westward—
the wind, too, rises and hurries.
How much can dream
be driven out
despite the wisdom
of hardship and habit?

4

The snow is cleared here.
The sun hesitates, returns,
and, upon the frost-flowered stones
where the animals are lain, blazes.
All there will be to save
will be the burden of this light,
gratuitous and fickle, this light struggling
out from under the lowering skies.

Some days there will be fair weather.
Some days it will be enough.

GRANDMOTHER AT THE DRESSMAKERS'

for Bonnie Thurston

———

A bolt of heavy, cobalt gabardine,
      shot with silver and scarlet threads,
      lay across the cutting table.
It was July. The overhead fan threw slow shadows
      upon the patterned, tin ceiling.
The neckline of Grandma's cotton housedress
      had grown dark with sweat.
The street outside, Mulberry, was empty—it was that hot.
Grandma, however, made lists and did not move from them.
A few minutes, that's all.
I did not chafe too much at the familiar words
      heard in grocery, at the neighbor's fence,
      though always
      my hand was tugging at her sleeve.
Bored, yes, but content enough, able
      to wait for the promises: lemonade, ice cream, cookies.
It was to be an elbow's length longer than the yardstick.
There was tracing paper, thimbles, tweezers, bodkins,
      and pinking shears with their intriguing teeth.
I took it all in, bothering and circling the women
      with questions, anxious to know as much here
      as I did in the barnyard with Father.

It was not poetry. Not yet. But it was life as I knew it
and I was keen to know it more, to keep gathering
as I did berries and stamps and pebbles,
to see what rarities might show up, sparkle, and speak:
muscled cloth, scissor slash, and how precision
might be wedded to beauty,
to be the kind of gatherer
who would not starve
even when my clothes grew thin
and words become the coinage of surrender.

SOMEWHERE

The floor is strewn with papered boxes, great flowers of
glossy ribbons, twisting snakes of pastel lacings. That
would be Mother's sweet work, hiding his father like this.
Eighteen years they lived in this house. He searches every
one, whispering his father's name, patiently, persistently.
The ashtrays are still on the mantle, his feed cap still hangs
on a nail in the barn, paint-speckled shoes grow green in
the basement. He should be able to find him . . . some-
where. The new pup is perplexed. She only knows rabbit
and squirrel and ground-meat dinners in gravy. She's never
smelled Tanbark and whiskey, Prince Albert and the way
coffee darkened the smell of Father's sweat. He keeps
opening the boxes, tearing out the knots, slitting free the
scotch tape on this hot holiday in July, corn knee-high, no
breeze, crows calling beyond the window, futilely, for rain.
He keeps listening for the sound of his father's trapped
voice, the tenderness he knows he would hear could he
find him. The reindeer are gone from the roof, the cradle
empty, the Advent calendar stored away until next season.
Is this how it always ends, another Christmas of hand-knit
socks, licorice, and a single orange? But surely, surely she
would not have taken such care to wrap a dozen empty
boxes?

POSTCARD

———

1

A postcard arrived from San Francisco telling of Medjool dates and fresh calamari. It wasn't from anyone they knew. Still, the snow kept falling and the postmistress said it had to mean something.

Tom had placed his pencil as a bulging bookmark in the thirteenth chapter of First Corinthians and gone out to feed the cats, grab more wood for the fire. They say the icicle must have measured near three feet, pierced his shoulder like butter, just nipping his heart—blood loss, shock, cold—anyone's guess what with the doctor away in Alabama, but it's clear Tom's not in real good shape, and Virgil, the dentist, is a whole lot better at teeth. Still, he'll see what can be done. You know Tom was in love with that Fletcher girl. Too bad, but there you are, the arrow doesn't always find the heart it's aimed for.

Meanwhile, the dogs are barking. Must mean Ruth's home from Richmond with the gossip. But it will be hard for her to beat that postcard. Squid like in the movies! Hard to imagine a day goes by without some miracle or another.

2

Tom died on Tuesday. The surprise that it wasn't sooner.
They all remember what Virgil tried to do for poor
Ruth. Walks with a limp to this day as she carries the
gossip from here to St. Peter's. But Tom's at peace, they
will say, some of them will. Others make a vow to stay
clear of Virgil.

It's coming on another storm.

They taste good.

What's that?

Dates . . . you know.

*Oh, yes, I know. Maybe six inches by tomorrow—you
believe it?*

Could be. I remember Tom liked dates.

He did . . . that's a fact.

The snow's falling again. And rain tomorrow. Someone
will be right about that. Maybe Virgil. He still feels bad
though no one blames him. It's like snow, like rain. It's
just like that water going under that bridge . . .

SEVEN LEAGUE BOOTS

And as it ever shall be . . .
        so here, the red
        car flashing past, silvery
        fins, a blur, its wake awakening me
        to when I was,
        long ago, on a corner
        in Fort Wayne, and the sky
        just then lifting
        over the night's ravaged horizon of storm,
        lifted itself into blue blazes, and men
        were soon wiping their brows,
        miserable in their Sunday best
        slouching out from First Christian,
        and I thought I knew
        something then about
        Sunday afternoons and the peace
        of quiet, and the steady breeze, and Mother
        lying down in the bedroom,
        and Pop coming out from there after
        smoking a rare cigarette
        with that faraway smile
        I would only see then,
        and on those nights he fell asleep
        reading Richard Halliburton

while the fights
droned on in the background,
and perhaps he never did
look sharp as the commercial urged,
but he did look,
pretty much,
like a goddamned god to me.

AUNT HELEN

———

Behold, I stand at the door, and knock.

The heavy shears lay on the oak table where a folded
square of gingham had lain earlier. And before that our
dinners. I was home to help get in the last bales. Beyond
the barn lot, the clanking rhythm of the old rake kept
turning the hay into rippling rows. Elmer and Merl would
finish, and the neighbor boy serve to fetch the undertaker.
And me, well, I had this other job now: to keep watch. The
early moon held its curved blade under the black clouds
and the pressing worry was rain and dark. It would be a
race with lanterns at the end. Helen was old, had been old
a long time, but would be no older now. When Elmer had
lifted her head gently from the fabric spread there on the
table, the only stain was sweat. She'd not soiled herself, nor
fallen from the chair. "She always worked hard and loved
new cloth." He drew her head into his shoulder as he knelt
beside her and was fastidious as he loosened her swollen
fingers from those scissors. "Old girl had good innings."
This said to me, slowly, as if telling me the secret of the fif-
ty-one years of marriage, and maybe he was. Then he was
off, back to the fields. And before the undertaker arrived,
I was to sit with her, give her quiet company: hay-making
weather too good to waste on death. Aunt Helen would

have approved. The only dissent came in the mystery
within which I sat alone waiting, waiting for someone
who knew more than I did. What lay there now so still,
upon that table where her hands had scissored gingham,
hacked meat, kneaded bread, beat batter into jellyrolls and
cookies, what lay there now I had no sure words for. And
this velvet Jesus knocking on Hunt's obstinate door there
on her kitchen wall—no words for Him, either, though it
should have been easy enough to let a god come in and sit
a spell. They say He only asked to break bread. It should
have been easy, but as long as death lay so motionless
there where life had been so busy, I stayed silent, deter-
mined to puzzle it all out myself before I would say *amen*.

II
―――――

Leave the door open for the unknown, the door into the dark. That's where the most important things come from, where you yourself came from, and where you will go.

–Rebecca Solnit,
A Field Guide to Getting Lost

EVIDENCE

A rusted trestle high over the gully,
    Norfolk and Western running out of town,
    out of steam, out of here forever.
Coltsfoot spangles the graveled bed.
Spears of broken glass glint, go dark under clouds.
Deftly as it can, the unwary pup
    limps home, a whimper
    outside the arguments
    inside.
What goes unnoticed will disappear.
Cats know how to do it better.
A child knows only how to ask.

FINDING THE LOST

We lean our elbows on the table and look out
      over the pallid lawn:
      a pool of white chrysanthemums
      below the glossy rhododendron thicket.
Cricket shadows ebb and flow with their bony music.
Autumn simmers where the heat lightning
      pieces together distant clouds.

Inside, we explore scrapbooks filled
      with curling black pages, broken tabs,
      and a host of black and white ghosts:
      an un-retrievable sustenance.
Still, we study, pore over the faces,
      look for bits and pieces, crumbs, a sip
      from the mead of memories
      to loose even a thin resurrection of spirit.

Eventually we let the sun go, draw the blind,
      light our few candles,
      imagine some kind of ritual, dream
      later into the night a trail of broken branches.
The owls watch with the tiniest of bones
      crunching under their yellow beaks.

Perhaps, in the morning, when the old light seems new,
    the frost on the window
    will bear an arcane script one of us will translate
    with a kiss and a finely hewn promise of fidelity.
We know we have to find our way back
    to save ourselves, our kin, the little shrews.

The sky pours toward us, purple, and bearing for us the few
    solicitous words left to speak what
    we hadn't known was spoken
    when our forebears had stood straight
    in that black and white future . . .
    free of us,
    free of menace,
    and the only bones
    their own familiar, arthritic ones.

HOW WE GO MISSING

The white balloon,
a child's fist
snagged on a currant bush.

Someone's out looking for jewels,
runic twigs, the fortune
leaves escaped from their cookies.

An old sailor coughs
on the park bench.
Another discovers a murderer
below the fold.

Beyond the lane
the sun is level with the tree line.
Soon the silhouettes of dusk will lie there.
Birds carry their last songs into the busy shadows.

CARRION CHANCE

———

It felt like the warning
Of what I feel now.

—Lord Byron

1

And so the black-faced vultures flew.
They flew in circles high, and higher,
and so I knew you were there, made new
somewhere near, changed, under a changing sky.

We had grown apart, had gone our ways,
ways to freedom, and within our schemes
we felt we'd known as much as anyone any day,
but paths shift, anchors weigh. Adrift, we dreamed

of more . . . but *almost love* a corruption, a violent
unraveling that stalks what would have been enough;
so you wandered, dangerously, map-less, relentless,
left me crying name after name, sometimes yours,
    blind man's bluff.

2

Facebook without faces: Still, we knew and arranged
a reunion, wooded paths we'd followed before,

appropriate, halfway in so many Dantean ways, strange
as our parting. Dreaded you more now after our wars.
But here, shouting, losing you again, to a sky of black
   flames,
to these scavengers of bone, these last adjudicators . . .

It was always the wrong word anyhow: *love* become *nice*.
I had tried hard and, very cautiously,
thrown the wrong dice.

WHERE NO ONE ELSE CAN GO

With a fistful of white violets the girl
is left inside the screaming house.
When the thinning moon opens the blue clouds,
kettles of restless shadow disperse
into the mirrors her mother
had placed so carefully in every corner.
Misguided perpetuations of eternity,
they glow like fading TVs at midnight.

With mauve lipstick the girl sketches faces on every one.
When the cops come, she grips that blue man's fingers
and leads him deeper and deeper into the house, a house
he would've sworn was only two up and two down.
He has never seen so much broken glass
and for every fragment she has a story and a name:
Thomas slit his throat with a scythe, Maureen
was done in with these horse pills, choking and silent,
and the piglets were burned alive after the farmer finished
reading the letter from the bank—notarized, a nice touch.

How do you know these things, he asks.
But she says nothing, only lifts one of the violets
as the lady without shadows continues
snipping silently beside her,

and she, only a girl, keeps dancing
out of the way, turning and un-turning, remembering the
    speed
with which the little things of God go bouncing
against those paper-thin walls of childhood
where she has heard
everything there is
to know about evil,
about the disguises people wear
to trick you into thinking like them, to imagine
you are invisible
just because they know
how to make you disappear.

PIETÀ

These fragile leaves
give the best light,
silent torches of gold frost
lighting the setting dusk-light.
Off and below the curve of the hill
the poplars rise to meet her.
She comes to see them,
their incendiary fall,
their passage as certain
as that of his who was her own.
She comes each day
to learn at this place,
where the hollow cleaves the hill,
to learn by heart her remembering
of where, in the slow, burning light,
they, these old poplars
on this old ground, where they go.
She would follow
as far as Hamlin stone
into its dark hold of lives
if death's piping would show her reason,
would follow now into this wood,
under these poplars, their slow fire,
go into the rain, go in this cold

into the heart of what's lost
too soon, too early
to rise, to come again
quick and light.
She would go to find
if under these leaves,
their last light, there were something, some clue
could give back the path
her life led before, could return
its light, its comfort.
But what light there is
fades, lifts tall,
regular shadows
returning to her only the weather,
the season, the minutes,
the wind, a drench of fog,
the road, a lash of distances,
the earth, a maze of hills,
and there, in those hills,
their ancient stone,
will be the only succor,
their time alone
long enough
for forgetting and remembering,
for remembering
the way the leaves were golden
mirrors the evening the news came,

for remembering, as she must,
as she did then, the quality of stone,
its holdfast against life, herself,
remembering to return, make the fire,
make, in its gentle shadows, over stone
a light, a meal,
and afterward reach toward sleep,
remembering in the cold room
to pull the comforts
to her chin, the quilted swirl of crazy pieces,
their twining branches of cloth,
like a twining tracery of leaves,
these few leaves at the last
the only light, a glimmer,
vouchsafed,
of the last light.

A MOON SOMEWHERE ELSE

———

Ice roses on a white bank,
      translucent vases of blood-milk—
      the deer are cautious, skittish.
Owls un-scroll in their muffled Morse
      all the meaning there is for the coming hours.
In the distance, a train.
God forbid a stranger should find his way here.
The barns are all empty.
Even the nicker of the dead horse has vanished.
It will be enough to remember
      everything as it is.
And so he promises to make up nothing but the truth.

PINK LADIES

Three red roofs crown a gray hill.
The moon is ringed by an opalescent halo
     within which a single red star shines.
A girl in a polka-dot shift has just
     lifted herself from her bicycle.
She has cut her smile from a photograph
     of her cousin, the sexy one,
     who sees a different boy every weekend.
     It will get her into trouble if she's not careful.
Jim, who loves puzzles, goes to work daily
     where, under the factory's shadow,
     he awaits his reprieve from destiny.
     It should be easier than this.
But his parents loved him and did
     most of the right things parents should do.
Monday, he doesn't go to work but
     cups his mother's ruby in his hands
     and remembers how she had had a polka-dot shift
     with a little black ruffle under the bodice.
The girl rides by just as the whistle blows.
He feels the breeze of her passing.
He remembers the way the breeze blew by
     when he had raced home from school to find
     his father dead, almost asleep, peaceful, a quick
     stroke with no regrets. His father had loved

Pink Ladies, a sharp, sweet apple
that grew on his uncle's farm.
Tuesday, Jim finds an orchard near Romney
and buys a peck of old apples, pink, blushing.
He's holding one in his hands and dreaming about love.
Wednesday night, late, as he walks the dog, he looks up,
finds himself encircled by the moon's ring
and a single star, glinting its primeval red light,
and in this mist, well, almost pink.
Tonight, the world will come to an end once more
and he will rejoice to think
he has this much with which to start over.
Already he's planning a village where the men
are all able and the women love to sing,
and like a toy train lay-out he'll have all the roofs
painted red. Almost pink. And the girl will grow
up and be called Persephone
and some day come home to love only him.
You wait—everything will work out just fine.
Jesus will climb down off the roof, his nail apron
honest and dirty
as he holds the ladder for the others.
And the kisses she gives as she looses
her pink polka dots, one by one,
will set fire to the darkness, will be for Jim,
and him alone, sweet as apples.

WHERE THEY CAN'T FIND US

———

I told them I was undeserving
    and must decline. They were pleased.
The parade would proceed—"outstanding triumph"
    remain in gilt upon the scarlet pennants.
A new name would, of course, be drawn
    from a shallow hat.
So many were thrown, a heavy
    confetti of head-ware.
I was escorted, contorted in rope, made sport of,
    any port in a storm not of
    my choice, my new motto, but I was
    disinclined to
    swim.
Took a chance, *a little old Case knife*.
I could see the warren of alleyways ahead,
    somewhere my new home, somewhere beyond here.
It was considerate.
I was to be *lost*.

And she . . . ?
Was unexpected.
We took turns in the rain
    believing it was
    our luck
    to be leaving town.

Between us we had about half the puzzle.
Hers had been a pumpkin and mine a hearse.
A clean get-away, nonetheless, for us both.

I'm assured the weather will continue.
Even the mice have umbrellas.
That they had had elaborate plans for us
        we had been certain.
I told her about the hats.
She was not surprised.
She told me about shoes and clocks.

There is sometimes a sun behind the third cloud
        to the right.
We sketch the map of true witness.
We may dry out and take up farming,
        hire a few mice, pretend we know
        what we're doing.
We'll raise ducks and vegetables and children
        wise enough to keep their hats on,
            and tell them to avoid parades and any approbations
                but our own tender kisses.
The lullabies are brewing even now.
She takes two sugars and I take one.
We are at peace with the lopsided.
Even now one of us is tipping
        into the other's arms.

III

———

Be grateful for anything that still cuts. Dissonance is a beauty that familiarity hasn't destroyed yet.

—Richard Powers, *Orfeo*

NOT QUITE HAPHAZARDLY

The questions
are not answerable,
but you are.

—Peyton Houston

Because bitterness is feeding the children,
because the crowds before the caskets have shrunk,
because fear nurtures our neighborliness,
because the leaves are falling not quite haphazardly,
falling in a light as golden as oak and poplar
against a sky as many-chambered as crystal,
because we have been here, under this,
and not seen,
and been here seeing nothing for so long
that our lying about it has grown brilliant as Technicolor,
because there are times when we get another chance,
when the sky breaks, crumbles,
rains down in great slashings,
the leaves gushing along the gutters
in slurries of faded pigment,
because it has happened once
and we remember to look, to reach for it again
thinking it is sky, that it is rain,
that it will be enough, and isn't,

but we remember
because the crying beyond the fence is of children
and the blood seeping below the gate is near,
because near is not so far
and the distances have come closer,
and because we can still find the crack in the wall,
because we open the gate every day,
because we can see between the floorboards,
still find a place to stand,
because we know fence and gate and floor,
know the futility of avarice, know we have tasted sweet,
and green, and fruit, and carousels, and even childhood,
because we have also known bitterness,
have never lost its taste,
and because the future has come again,
and because we have come near it looking,
looking for a lens
clear as one of those once-upon-a-time days
when we had seen, deep, and beyond time,
because now we hear a voice
and move, turn toward it,
because it is near,
because there is sky and rushing water,
because there are yet flowers and stones,
because there are leaves, falling, not quite haphazardly . . .
because there are times when we get another chance.

THESE

for Jerry

———

These are not lucky charms. These
are bits of bone and sinew. Home
from the war, he pressed them into my hand.
I said, "Thanks," and he walked away. Far
away he had been. Steep valleys,
hot mountains of war, highs
stolen when the moon was bright
and the enemy shy. "See,"
he once said on leave, "there
won't be much left of me." I know
that now, holding his hand in mine,
charms are not enough. Prayer
names names. We try them. One
after another. Repeat after each, "Lord,
have mercy, Lord, Lord . . ."
Names have memories. I wear his now.
Pray it as if he hears.

FUCKED

He is deaf from the whining scream of the chainsaw and is sweating under the thinning, November sun. There must have been some way to avoid this hellhole in the Middle East. When he had seen the pictures on the screen last night, something had knotted in his belly. But here, at least, this morning, the work felt good, the bright, interior heart of the tree exposed like this. Fuck politics. There were wormholes. Some people liked them in their furniture. Antique. He was fifty-nine years old. And lately it felt old. Antique. Christ, what he wouldn't give for a beer and a chance to get laid by that girl at Tommy's. She was a bright thing. He'd vote the bastards out of office if any other bastards would do any better. The white house down below had rung the cops once about his chain-sawing on Sunday. Fuck the neighbors and their Sunday. Fuck the neighbors and their lament about the old elm. Fuck everyone. What was it his son had said in that poem. "*Fuck* was a strong word, an Anglo Saxon word, a good word that gets the job done." He was sharp, that boy of his, despite his politics. Funny how the kid could be so sharp and dumb all at once. How anyone could believe in those sissy, liberal assholes, but worse, he began to think, how could anyone believe anything at all? Maybe all he needed was to introduce his son to Sheila down there at

Tommy's. Maybe that was all anyone ever really needed. It was worth a try. One more cut and he'd have the hour in and enough firewood for a month. It felt good. But, Jesus, those little kids. That was what bugged him. Little kids, parts of their bodies just strewn across the ground like windblown trash. And our boys did this? Something was fucked . . . big time.

THE INNOCENT

The iron gate opens into a field of snowmen lively with
sticks and carrots and their button-eyes of coal. No one
asks who put them there, so eager are we to mingle, to get
acquainted. A crow older than the far mountains calls to
us in his misery. It was not his choice to stay behind here
where color holds for him no advantage. The sun has been
told to stay away by this army of cold warriors whose
stolidity brooks no compromise. It obeys according to
the terms of a treaty made when the old was new and far
away. We walk further into this stage set for a December
pageant of badly dressed and skinny children, orphans and
waifs from Basra and Tirkut, Tamil Nadu, Aceh, Kobane,
Bethlehem, children whose lives are to be cut short—of
this we are reminded in this white garden beyond the
black gate. Perhaps it is the cold. Adam lived in other
forests besides Eden. Somewhere beyond the Tigris it is
snowing even now. And on a beach somewhere in Turkey
that little boy . . .

TIME TRAVELER IN GREENVILLE, OHIO

—

. . . to know more about this globe than
anyone else ever has.

—Lowell Thomas

The bald man sits, hands pursed like his lips, eyes glis-
tening, reels of memory spinning in a narrow cavern of
theater light—here and there he can read the credits
that tell his life. Overhead the tin ceiling offers change-
less weather and around him the bar flickers its neon
noise. The dog chained to the back door chews his leash.
Soon it will erupt into freedom like a moth into bright
oblivion. It's coming too fast, his heart racing. The man
stumbles back to his room, tries to keep pace with the
movie channel as together they plummet through time.
Where are his meds? A locomotive coughs outside the
roundhouse. He looks up, sees Lowell Thomas behind
the front lines interviewing the crocodiles: *Good evening,*
everybody. The man's reading has become a race. He works
at the words: best boy, make-up, casting, rendering, gaffer,
dolly grip. . . . At last the dog's teeth tear through and
he's off, free, running a straight line for home, straight
home—an eight-lane interstate in his way. The landmarks
blur for both. The man begins grabbing great fists of
words, stuffing them into his mouth like pills, little black

pills, and although this unexpected largesse is lethal, he smiles as he echoes the screen voice trailing through the jungles of 1943: *So long until tomorrow*. The bar's runway is too slick for any landing and the dog flips and soars, up into the Nakajima skies that break open in a flak-fever of fireworks. The man despairs when the reel blisters into the rapid slap-slap of interruption. But he holds on, eyes closed, holding the TV to his chest like a lover, the bloodied carcass whimpering, the newsreel talking like it was *this* dog and Lowell Thomas had come back to Greenville, Ohio, for this very reason . . . to kneel as flowers flame over the crypt of a friendly gaffer, and for the hundredth time hear again: *so long . . . until tomorrow*.

BROKEN

A perturbation in the dream grid, a knife in the socket,
   time's chaperone screaming,
   and so the trepidation of dressing
   assails the child you can still almost recall
   lingering, soiled and
   beaten with belt and
   fist and
   the most marvelous curses.

Under the bank of gray windows the traffic flows
   in threads of silver and splash.

Later in the morning, when you walk the bright path,
   your map is still new, legible,
   and safely in your pocket.
The rain slips easily from somewhere overhead.

You had heard the man mumbling his prayers.
Without an umbrella, you had handed him
   your comb, for his hair. Laughed.
A good joke, but he didn't smile—
   maybe he was just about to get it
   when the toe of your boot went up his ass.

The jobs never last beyond noon or, more rarely,
        the occasional sundown.
The docks were more dependable last month.

You are capable and in love with your zany generosity.
Men. Women. Equal opportunity player is how you see it.
When they hand over the goods,
        or suck you off as instructed,
        you have a rich lexicon of cordial
        courtesies to offer.

When the beach has worn away
        the last whisperings of light,
        you can almost feel
        your heart lift
        out of its cage
        toward something.

You caned a man for his wallet but had been
        deferential in doing so,
        expressing both gratitude and respect,
        but when he forgot to thank you,
        you drove your stick
        through the soft part of his belly.
You miss that cane, and now you can't sleep.

Still, you get up each morning and come to the table
        expecting something a little more
        in return than cash.
You expect a more sufficient appreciation.
Perhaps a song with nightingales providing the chorus.
Perhaps a kiss—nothing is so long ago as that,
        or as valuable.
Perhaps this, the white light shimmering over the canal
        just before you lift your fists, those stones
        of ancient anger,
        and splash the still mirror,
        make it flash and thunder,
        make it all real again,
        what was done there in that old room
        so long ago and always as near
        as these hands you still carry
        clenched in your pockets,
        ready, and broken.

NOT WITH A BANG

———

*Whenever I hear the word culture, the first thing I do is
reach for my gun.*

—Hanns Johst, Nazi playwright

We'd shown up at Tommy's Place, Oak and Main. He'd
not stop talking about his trip to Guadalajara. The
mariachi bands and whores. The frisson of danger, the
cartels, and, well, he'd met someone who'd actually seen
a pit full of bones. We were his better friends, eager for
stories, the tight dresses, the imbroglio over nuance and
silks entertaining, and blood the chaser adding an edge we
appreciated perched on barstools in that Friday cocoon
of paycheck boozers. But it got to be too much drink and
smoke and suddenly I was disappearing, a jeep hell-bent
for speed through a jungle of mirrors in a third or fourth
world hard-wired for truth and the alcohol was gone
and worse was seeing you nailed spread-eagled on a box
car waiting for justice and all our hands empty and you
wouldn't stop laughing and I said I'd have to kill you if you
didn't stop.

My heart breaks that desperation cousins such stories.
We're all chasing trains now. And sober, too, the seconds
ticking, the hornets descending in organized clouds, like

smoke under orders from Goering still reaching for his
gun and cyanide. It's coke and sports and all the rest,
Joaquin Guzman and Christian quarterbacks feeding the
underbelly of America. What we've all done with our
lives—kindling, that's all. You can't tame leeches with
Bibles. And none of us could sleep forty nights in our
backyards, let alone befriend stones, make peace with
hunger, love an angel for more than her body. It's suddenly
over, this American game of boys. The stories at Tommy's
were always about the wars over there when really the
flames were wrapping themselves around the hearts here
where we play make-believe with undeniable and perfect
skill. Someone says to duck our heads and we all stand
and stare. It's that kind of whimper, that kind of not so
happy ever after.

ANTI-MONOTONY

———

Popcorn and a gray pear and a lizard on a leash—they
had returned him to the land where bronze light held
everything under its close and ubiquitous lens. A bear,
manacled by the monotony of cotton candy and circuses,
could only dream there had once been a green season
with green light in a free wilderness and something other
than castles filled with dungeons. He didn't like lizards
or popcorn or dressing like a man. He didn't like going
backward and forward every day sliced between the three
panels of the world. He didn't ask to be here. He didn't ask
for everything to go on being the same day after day. His
brain was burning with desires, with longing, with dreams.
. . . Even now there is a trail of smoke. If only he could take
off these gloves, remove his collar, piss on the flag—he
would show them how blood un-cogs the wheel. But
another day passes and the season refuses to budge and
the pear continues to dangle by its slender stem, neither
dead nor alive.

NORMAL

In the beginning we come in after the big bang, after the six days, after the dream, after the good was still suspended, inviolate, among the clouds, a hot air balloon filled with hope and surety. Not much later, in a room next door, the creation gets going in earnest as she juggles the proto-types of creatures as yet unnamed, stomps her foot in anticipation of their dancing, while the three-headed scarecrow in motley straitjacket begs an extra dose of mercy. She may be listening, but she cannot see his suffering, only sense there is a ripple now in the distant sky where memory has been seeded, that covenant whose remembering lifts us from the floor and its tipped and tumbled boxes. *This side up* if you are to see through the mayhem to where the bow is strung between the clouds. Bees are in the honeycomb, sweet and misery ordered together, puzzles yet to come. *If I knew the way, I would take you home.*

VEHICULAR

You come round a curve, the blind crest of a hill
and suddenly there are these two lives waiting
for you, comedic and tragic together, waiting
for you who are to be an instrument
from the ancient Greek stage,
you who are to be as innocent as we ever are with chance
and the bad luck of being human.

You see a cobalt-blue Duster jacked up
in the near middle of the road.
You see two statues that could be people.
You even see the Holsteins in the distance, the white barns,
the last light of day, the curious moment within which
this new story has to begin.

The seconds divide themselves slowly at first,
offering time its true nature.
The drunk boyfriend, cell to his ear, continues
to stand, back to the action.
The girl straightens her shoulders and then,
wide-eyed, slow-mo, she runs . . .
runs the wrong way on the wrong side
of that wrong road on that wrong day.

The Duster was a solid.
The girl was a blur of time frozen.
The boy was peripheral.
You were driving the company's pickup, a Chevy S10.
You were thinking things through, being careful
and human, being as good
as the unlucky innocent ever can be,
when the seconds began accelerating
and you were dropped into instinct, and swerved
to avoid a collision with that blue Plymouth, swerved
into time, that blur, that little motion, that fleeting last
second of a life, the blood and bone of it, and it was
only a small sort of bump, quiet, and was behind you
as quickly as it had been before you,
behind you where the new seconds began
without any screaming to tick the silence forward
into your own time and place that gathers
around you now at night,
alone, without anything so solid as steel and bone,
as even the slender words in the town obituary
that would carry her name, without anything
to anchor you
but this moment that refuses to move beyond that glance
back over your shoulder where the living die
without your impatient wish to be perfectly forgiven
even this . . . your almost perfect innocence.

IV

———

The possession of knowledge does not kill the sense of wonder and mystery. There is always more mystery.

—Anaïs Nin

IT WAS TOLD

It was told this way, once upon a time.
It had to do with God, a boundary
somewhere to the north.
And an old king no one remembered
except those who loved
            and those who hated him.
The many birds were threading the morning with their
    little stories.
Nothing comes back to haunt them.
They are god-less and innocent.
A peaceful morning. Dew glistening on a lawn.
Still, no one lifts a spoon, turns a page, without listening.
Soon clouds return to lower themselves into this old valley.
Fire appears in clusters of bright baskets,
            smoke spreading along the streets.
It will be hard to see when you go out.
She has reread the marginalia in Grandmother's Bible.
She has rehearsed her sums.
She has rinsed the chamomile from her hair. It shines.
Like thunder the drums were beginning again. Echoing.
The river ran its large silence under the bridge
and waited to be fed.
Yesterday, from the top of the street, the barricades had
    held till noon.

No one has yet washed the brown stains away.
It was an old town and had known such stories before.
Still, this was not on anyone's script:

>the young father, deaf and unarmed;
>his favorite cat; the pretty house; the lovely maid.

We should be writing fairy tales with all this blood.
Even the soldiers come out from their tents to weep.
Their silver tributaries burn a map where they crisscross
    the parade grounds.
But the hide and seek will resume, has already, is now.
She ducks her head below the clematis at the garden gate,

>steals her way down the alley carrying cherries for
>   Grandmother.

She would like to return alive and with her curls still
    springing, shining.
Some of them claim God with stony hearts and brilliant
    tongues.
Others keep him hidden in pockets full of beads and cash.
It remains enough to feed the newspapers:
The children. The hate.
War makes some exaggerate the screaming and the noise.
With a rifle it is more often a dull thud, the bullet
    suddenly slowing down
inside flesh and sinew, stopping as it grates upon cartilage
    and bone.
Yet, although not loud, the whimpering is remembered.

In recent weeks the war has evolved:
assassination, torture, negotiation.
Almost every day there is a cease-fire meant to be broken.
Corpses get mistaken for piles of rags.
Rags get mistaken for scarecrows and dance
on the clotheslines of saints.
She gets lost in a lilac wood. The barbwire tears at her
  dress.
She is never seen again.
Did she get lost in hope?
Or did they bury her where the river slides
    its emerald caskets into the sea?

COLD MORNING

———

Near sun-break, a drone,
deep-grown, spreads
through the limbs, branches, all
ragged foils to this
storm music falling
upon the unsuspecting
morning, the hillside above
limning the petals, this tracery
lifting the light, and my fingers,
splayed against the window,
translucent, cooling stars, whimsy
melding the out there with here,
the blood hours, the homing
reach to wake song
from frost and flame.

STONE

It must have been last night the moon threw
        down this stone, or the earth
        let it float loose, up, and returned it to light.
A stone as silent as a new-dug grave.
A stone with a history longer than even the endless cycling
        of the little stream here behind me
        racing a nameless forest to the sea.

Imagine how long the things of this earth must sometimes
    wait to be heard.
And yet this stone squats upon this green turf in its snug
        and impermeable white skin,
        as patient as a fox in the lap of the Buddha,
        while the thin noon of March slowly
        lifts over our tawdry certainties.

Nearby cardinals are warming up their spring song,
        tossing it between the branches of a slender hemlock.
They are the apples of winter.
They are bright-feathered engines of blood and wonder.
They are here to speak,
        to re-member the sentience of all things.
All I have to do is translate. I don't have to worry
        about getting it right. Eternity is for that,
        and this day

I only plan to look over its gates,
part the lower branches,
squint, listen to what whispers,
cradle this stone in the palm of my hand
and speak with it as if it were resilient metaphor
willing to accept my give and take,
as capable of every term in life's taxonomy as I am.

I am tossing it back and forth between my left
      and my right hand.
And now, right now, I am tossing it to you, and will wait
      for you to toss it back with your own understanding
      that this moment has been,
      as we might some day be ourselves,
      silent, small, and perfect
      as a stone, patient,
      and listening,
      as I am,
      for what comes next.

WINTER INTO SPRING

———

. . . for here there is no place / that does not see you.

—Rilke

Where floods carried off the late snows,
the rumpled, pale fold of late summer's lush riot—
joe pye and goldenrod, ragweed and yarrow—
a record of the torrential passage that spread
up from the creek twenty yards each side,
the young elms and locusts alone
withstanding the imprint of the water's passing
and tressed now like bridesmaids
with the detritus of all that came unanchored.

For color there are stones
trailing their emerald threads of cress
and the bank's grasses,
wan and brittle,
and the sky, a blue
so light with sun
all the under-branching of brush
shimmers silver.

One split and rotting log is furred
with a spidery moss along which runs
a three-foot snake of red bramble:

even days under the pounding pressure
of the waters' pull to ocean
has not robbed it of its tiny thorns—
grass-blade thin and sharp.

In the creek itself insects as big as a pinhead
wander in and out of rocky pools, rocks starred
with pewter-wooden coins of lichen.
A thin, wheezing trill falls
from the pale warbler invisible
in the bright shining overhead,
and I shield my eyes,
try to see if this singing
can again weave
winter into spring.

LATE SEPTEMBER

Far up the south pasture, bristly and sharp now,
a golden fox nestles, patient
in a golden sun on a golden bank.
Night begins her slow walk over the next hill
carrying under her purple skirts
the book of chances
whose purpose is to pull everything together
like God would do were She and He here
to study perfection like we do
looking up the hill, up the sky,
up the page to where Blake draws a line
between Adam's first breath
and all the thunder to follow.

RECOVERIES

———

For just this moment, a sweep of swallows conflated
    with a lowering bed of rain-heavy clouds.

A deft toss of hail pebbles against the windows, then
    silence, then comes a blade of sunlight level
    with the horizon, then it's gone.

Where the stillness sleeps behind the closed door,
    a shadow stretches out as the light goes.

The clock with its tiny feet never quits chasing the moon
    sliding over the cattails and up the mountain
    into the night.

The morning comes, the skies swift and clear,
    and the ground sodden and glittering
    where the wren whistles its familiar trio of notes.

The creek continues, rushing and urgent in its push
    to join the somewhere seas
    heedless of time and responsibilities.

A wisp of white-yellow larch needles, wind-gathered,
      relax upon the skin of black water
      in the highland swamp.

With only a linen notebook in his pocket, he goes
      barefoot and believes only in the smaller miracles.

PETER'S MOUNTAIN

—

1

The night's fog pools now in this valley and
laps at the long sweep of mountain
twisting toward Virginia,
and with an early sun freeing shadows
and standing almost motionless,
slowly the fog coalesces
into the puff clouds
we named as children
dragon and castle,
elephant and snake and
Granddad's bearded face.

2

Later in a white tent, Beethoven's first Razumovsky
     quartet,
gentle and steady, a lulling surf in the viola,
a jaunty birdsong melody clear as water in the
     violins,
as if water could sing and light could be held,
and through the crack in the breeze-opened canvas
I see the far, green teeth of the ridgeline
rake the roiling bank

of cumulus from this blue July sky
and hold the light as if time itself
were learning patience and holding still
long enough for me to hold it here for you.

MONASTERY

———

Inside the cloistered quiet the men dug vegetables
  and listened for God
  and without any effort God came
  and sang for them in a wren suit
  and when God grew tired he lifted up the clouds
  and let sun dry the sweat on each worker's brow
  and then he lifted up all the green shoots
   just a little higher than the day before.
Upon such miracles was this order founded
  and, though it has been lost to time, some say
  they still follow their praxis in the greenwood
  there on the far side of that river
  across from which we all stand
  on the edge of believing.

JACKSON POLLOCK AND THE STARLINGS, MOUNDSVILLE, WEST VIRGINIA

———

The painting has a life of its own. I try to let it come through.

—Jackson Pollock

The starlings have again held their revival here.
The sidewalk below their power line pulpits
    is stippled with rose and ivory starbursts.
A few linger near yet this morning, whistling,
    as if they were unaware
    of their art, unaware
    of the limits of transcendence,
    unaware
    of the neighbors' lack of appreciation
    of mulberries, of art, of starlings with a purpose.

THE NEWS

for Jim Barnes

———

Under the awning,
in the blushing red shadows,
the old man reads the news
and sips at coffee until
a sparrow hops in off the street,
and the old man doffs his cap
and smiles, folds up his paper,
and stands. What I noticed
was how the bird watched
and did not fly.

CLARK HILL

———

Nature is a language, can't you read?
Ask me, ask me, ask me, ask me . . .

—Johnny Marr and Morrissey

The force of a dozen unrelenting springs
fractures the skin of this blue shale.
The cliff face weeps: rain, wind, and ice
smooth and crumble it. Change
is in the sharp gravel
below this mud-stone's sheer bank,
change, too, where driving above us
a harness of cloud pulls
green sheets onto a gray-plated sky.
Bird-black flags scatter overhead.
Straight pines open their arms to them.
Resolute, these proprieties of the green world.

YOU COULD LIVE

When the organ's crescendo ascends the high sanctuary, and
the walls seem to shimmer with the glorious remembrance
of battle, then you notice the little bat flit, for just a moment,
out from the shadows, and then back again. The stained
glass grows dull. Perhaps the cold front bearing its winter
load of rain has arrived. Someone is coughing. Someone else,
irritatingly, has re-opened their program, and you note again
how loud words on paper can be when they are unwanted.
The composer's name you have forgotten, but it's okay. For
a moment, just a moment, you had seen, could see over the
hill to where the celebrations were begun. She would be in
the streets waiting, waiting to welcome them all, but espe-
cially you. You had been brave. Once upon a time the rains
held off, the mail come with dispatch bearing just the right
message, and no shadows between yourself and your reward.
She would be holding a small, black handkerchief, lifting it
up, ready to wave, ready to fly. There would be a blessing in
the Mary chapel of the south transept. And did you notice
to your right, behind the old woman in her cloche, the one
who kept dabbing her eyes and whispering in French, did
you notice the battered pew left over from the bombing in
forty-one? The dash of a shadow, the flutter of a woman's
promise—are these enough? If you listen carefully, you can
almost hear the priest pronouncing the peace, joining their
hands, celebrating.

AND FLY

———

A pair of doves wade through the violet green
onto the gritty plain of newly hoed soil,
their mechanical bobbing as they peck
surprisingly graceful, fitting, and so keen
are they on their work I remain unseen
even as they draw closer with this foraging.

I lose track of time, lose it altogether,
seek words for the sheen of their gray-brown bodies
that seem not avian at all—head and back
more a skin with a blue stain on some feathers,
and in the right light an iridescence in the male,
black spotted wings, pearl-fleshed tails, and whether
I'd ever noticed their pink feet before, well, never

had I noticed as I do now, and so pause, and see,
and wish to understand beyond make-believe,
wish to communicate, to know how they go,
what they find with every peck, every second, know
is it fruitful this quest driven by these little
and jewel-perfect eyes? Wondering until,
with a thudding whinny, they spring, and lift, and fly.

BEYOND

Overhead, not the endless sky slipping
its massive, summer-white cumulus
through the gaps in the mountains
but trees, the arc and
leaf-flowering legs and arms of them,
upholding and centering that unbounded field.

Overhead, not the looping circles of vultures,
their desultory hunger unsated by the blue,
nor the whiskery, spirited breeze squeezed
through the bristled flanks of the distant cliffs;
not the crunch of gravel, nor the rattle of pocketed keys,
but the fragile insistence of a single wren, whistling.

Overhead, not heaven now, nor was it ever, but only this
looking to where things attach to moments
and so become as much eternity as I can stand,
even gravity's buoy to go some day
untethered from these stolid oaks
now upholding a single wren and the still, endless sky

that already's bleeding, slowly, into interstellar night
beyond clouds, beyond blue, beyond dark, beyond light.

WITH NO QUESTIONS

———

A steady sheet of rain is slipping through the woods,
    apple blossoms plastering the ground, the last snow,
      our first sorrow.
The gentle rush of the creek will be both dirge and lullaby.
A barred owl stutters deep within the beech grove.
My tea is cooling where it sits on the windowsill.
The rain lifts its last skirts over the ridge and leaves a
  dripping quiet in its wake

Suddenly, a tableau of four deer within the settling fog.
My dog barks now, belatedly, once, twice
    to let me know they're there—none of us very
      excited
    though the beauty of it, of them, still slows
    the reach of my hand for that solitary cup.

Meadow grass is dangling from one of their mouths, a
  damp, green bouquet.
When I stumble, drawing closer, their match-stick legs
    ferry them effortlessly down the rocky bank,
      their taupe velvet flanks soft as kisses, tough as
        weathered callous,
      their black eyes, their black noses, every part
      marvelously balanced.

They've stopped now inside some pocket of quiet below
   me.
We are all listening, each to the other,
      waiting for the next move in the universe.
And just here becomes the only place
      I know where time surrenders to itself
      and reverses what I think I know.

My tea is cold. The dog asleep. The rain gone.
And somewhere the owl is sliding the silence
      into the hidden trees of a deeper night
      with no questions about philosophy,
      with no questions at all.

READING NOTES

—

"Aunt Helen": Epigraph from Revelations 3:20

"Seven League Boots": Richard Halliburton was a popular travel/adventure writer of the 1920s and 1930s. His last book was *Seven League Boots*.

"Time Traveler in Greenville, Ohio": "So long until tomorrow" was Thomas's well-known sign-off phrase on his popular radio shows that ran for over four decades beginning in the 1930s.

"Normal": The last sentence is from Robert Hunter's lyrics for "Ripple" recorded by The Grateful Dead on the album *American Beauty*.

ABOUT THE AUTHOR

Marc Harshman grew up on a farm in east-central Indiana and has lived most of his adult life in northern West Virginia, where for many years he taught in the Sand Hill School, one of the last of the three-room country schools.

He was appointed the Poet Laureate of West Virginia in 2012 in recognition of his work as both a poet and children's author. Harshman's previous full-length collection, *Green-Silver and Silent*, was published in 2012. His four chapbooks of poetry include *Rose of Sharon*. His poems have appeared in many leading journals including the *Georgia Review*, *Quarterly West*, *Emerson Review*, *Shenandoah*, *Salamander*, *Poetry Salzburg Review*, *Gargoyle*, and many others in the US and abroad. His poems have been anthologized by The Kent State University Press, the University of Iowa Press, the University of Georgia Press, SPM Publications, Shepherd University, and the University of Arizona Press.

His thirteen children's books include *The Storm*, a Smithsonian Notable Book, and his newly released, *One Big Family*. His monthly show for West Virginia Public Radio, *The Poetry Break*, began airing in 2016.

CPSIA information can be obtained
at www.ICGtesting.com
Printed in the USA
FSOW03n1727010717
35715FS